The Circle of One

Kuumba Nia

The Circle of One

ISBN 978-0-9564194-4-6

A copy of this publication has been registered with the British Library.

Published by Blessings Book Publishing Limited– 2010 all rights reserved.

Cover Design by Blessings Book Publishing.

Printed by and bound by MPG Biddles Ltd, King's Lynn, Norfolk.

Blessings Book
PUBLISHING

Dedicated to:

To Phillip, Kaiesha & Kai, Joshua & Jasira

You have been my rock, my foundation, my core.

I am so glad to have shared the Circle with you.

Acknowledgements

The Circle of One is my small gift to the world.

I give it humbly and with love, in the hope that eventually, we will see the beauty of the Oneness of which we are all a part.

I am extremely grateful to the following people for helping me to make this book a reality. Only you will really appreciate the significance of your part in this journey.

Martyn Pentecost

David Francis

Pearl Thompson

Tom Evans

Lizzi Vandorpe

Contents

The Circle of One: Introduction

Preamble

This has been a strange journey.

The path that has set me to writing this book has been long and winding and full of challenge, and through it all, I knew that I had to write something down. Why? Because if I didn't, how would I know what I had learnt? How would I be able to share what I had learnt?

This book is the culmination of many experiences. Some of them have been good; some of them great; and some extremely painful. Yet all have brought me to where I am now; and for that I am truly grateful. Without them, I would not be the person I am today, and my life would be a lot less rich.

During those difficult times, what I did not appreciate was that a lot of the drama and pain had been of my own creation. The choices I had made, and the actions that I had taken had created the life I had. It was all of my own doing.

From where I am standing now, it seems so obvious; but things always do in hindsight. I would like to think that if I had had the tools and the 'know how' to make sense of it back then, I would have at least tried to avoid some of the 'stuff'. Yet the truth is

I would probably still have made the same decisions. What I believe however, is that if I had possessed the tool that I am about to share with you at that time, it would have saved me a lot of time and energy, and given me some understanding of the challenges that were being thrown up around me. It would have shown me some of the truths that I needed to tell myself, whether or not I was ready to hear them. But as I have always known, nothing happens before its time, and for me, that time is now.

The Circle of One is the distillation of my personal experiences, my work with clients and observations of people over the last six years, and I believe that now, more than ever, is the time to share it.

Not because it contains unique or original concepts. Indeed, the concepts in this book are not unique at all. They have been around for a long time. No. The reason why the time for this book is now is very simple: people are ready for it. You are ready for it. If you were not, you would not be reading this.

It may become apparent as you read on that this book is not written for the usual suspects. It is not for the ones with a PhD in Spirituality, or an in-depth knowledge of the esoteric. Nor is it for those who could speak for days on their quest for satori; the manifestation principles of the Law of Attraction; or even the seemingly unfathomable mysteries of quantum physics. This book is for the seekers; the curious; the ones who know there is another way, but have not found one that speaks to them, yet.

The Circle of One is for those who want a change in their relationships and their lives now. They know that there must be more to life than this, but they do not want to sit on top of a mountain waiting for it. They are tired of playing out the same relationship over and over again with different people, without ever really feeling happy or complete. They are worn out by the constant battles with parents or children that leave them feeling disconnected and isolated; and most importantly, they are exhausted by the effort of trying to gain approval and fulfilment through other people and wondering why they just cannot seem to get their relationships to work.

If you recognise any of these scenarios, either for yourself or those you know, then this book will help you to understand exactly what is going on in those relationships.

It will walk you through the simple and beautiful tool that is the Circle of One, and show you just how powerful it really is. Most significantly, it will show you how you can use it to heal your relationships and transform your life.

To do this, the Circle of One requires nothing but itself, your openness and your honest participation. It is not a cult or religion, and there is nothing that you have to believe. All that is required is that you suspend your disbelief and self sabotage long enough to gain from it.

Overstanding the big picture

How to use this book

For ease of reference, this book is presented in three parts. **Part One** looks at the social, cultural and energetic context to using the Circle of One, and takes you briefly through the journey that led to the birth of this book.

Part Two of the book gives an explanation of the way in which the Circle of One works, and its underlying principles. I felt it important to do this in order for you to gain an 'overstanding' of the big picture that we are involved in creating when we practice the Circle. Whilst these principles aim to give an understanding of how to apply and interpret the Circle of One, they can also serve as a guide for a way of life.

Part Three focuses on how we can use the Circle in our daily lives, and what we can do to continue our expansion when we start living the Circle. It takes us through the practical application of the Circle of One using a real life case study, and walks us through a step by step illustration of how you can use the Circle to work for you. This section also includes three additional case studies and some insights into to them; as well as developmental exercises that can be used when journaling or on their own.

There are a number of ways in which you can use this book, depending on what it is that you wish to achieve.

In the first instance, it can be used passively, with little or no input from you. By this, I mean that you can read it through, note the contents, and then put it down without practising the Circle or doing any of the exercises. When we read in this way, we often have the intention to go back and do the exercises later, but seldom do. This is by far the easiest way to use it, as it requires minimal effort in terms of engagement from you, or personal learning. Not surprisingly, this approach has limited benefits, as you only really experience the Circle on a superficial level.

Another way in which you can use this book is from a more intellectual perspective. From here you can examine the content, study the points raised, and intellectually assess the validity of it. When you carry out the exercises, you may do so purely from your head, becoming detached from the process, without allowing yourself to connect with your heart. Whilst this approach may give you a sense of safety and certainty, as your focus is likely to be more on thinking and less on feeling, it can rob you of the sense of connection and compassion that you need in order to grow emotionally.

What I believe to be the most useful and rewarding way to use The Circle of One is probably a combination of all of the above. From this perspective, you can choose to use the book actively, intellectually and intuitively; taking the time to let the ideas wash over you; to consider and critically evaluate without getting so bogged down that you miss the point, and to gain understanding at a heart level, that allows you to have compassion for yourself and others.

As the Circle of One is essentially a workbook written for practical application, it is of most use when the concept is applied to your daily life. Read it. Apply it. Learn from it. But however you choose to use this book, I trust that you will get exactly what it is that you need.

Part One: Context for the Circle

Energy Shifts: The Age of Aquarius

As I write this chapter, the world of the early twenty-first century is experiencing huge energy shifts. The ideas and institutions that we have long held in esteem and very much taken for granted, have been shaken to the core. So much so that there seems to be no doctrine that cannot be questioned or any possibility that cannot be considered.

The collapse of established transnational banking institutions like Lehman Brothers; the implementation of state sponsored financial recovery programmes in the US and Europe; and the global bid to shore up the foundations of capitalism itself, have all demonstrated the magnitude of the shift.

When I started writing this book, all I could think of was why now? What was the urgency to get this out now? Whilst my head was not always clear, my heart just knew that it was time. I was ready. People I knew were ready, and energetically, those parts of the world that had hitherto glorified the idea of individualism, isolation and disconnection, were now also ready to take on a new paradigm. Amidst the apparent chaos of war, famine and global economic meltdown, an energetic shift had taken place and we were ready to embrace a paradigm of connection, oneness and, dare I say it, love.

I was born in the 1960s, and one of the songs I remember hearing on the radio all the time was *Let the Sun Shine In*, or as most will remember it, the *Age of Aquarius*, from the musical *Hair*. The opening verse of the song began:

When the moon is in the Seventh House

And Jupiter aligns with Mars

Then peace will guide the planets

And love will steer the stars.

This is the Dawning of the Age of Aquarius!

Age of Aquarius! Age of Aquarius!

Now there are people out there far more qualified than I, who will tell you that the Age of Aquarius has not yet arrived, and may well give you an auspicious date, at some point in the future, when it will arrive. They may even tell you how long it will last, and what astronomical or astrological factors may contribute to this.

For me, the date is not important. What really matters here is not the specificity of the dates and times, but the characteristics that this age is said to exhibit. According to the song:

"Harmony and understanding
Sympathy and trust abounding
No more falsehoods or derisions
Golden living dreams of visions
Mystic crystal revelation
And the mind's true liberation

Aquarius! Aquarius!"

Harmony & Understanding

For the die hard cynics amongst you, this may seem like so much New Age nonsense. Yet if we stop for a moment and think a while, it would be hard not to conclude that the world today feels very different to perhaps twenty years ago; and not just a little different, but fundamentally so. We have seen the election of the first black president of the most powerful country in the world, massive earthquakes in Haiti, Chile and other parts of the globe; and it feels as if we are witnessing energetic shifts of such magnitude that the world may never quite seem the same again. And whilst some of the shifts may appear to be destructive, almost bordering on the apocalyptic in some cases, they do not feel to me as though they are occurring in order to give us more of the same. They do not feel to me like the doom and gloom of the 'last days', but as if they are making way for something new and exciting; something full of optimism and promise.

In the last decade, we have seen a tsunami that travelled half way across the world from Bali to West Africa; the increasingly frequent occurrence of floods in Bangladesh and other areas of the Indian sub-continent; the world-changing attacks on the World Trade Centre in the United States; and a global financial crisis that has thrown Western economies into massive recession. We have also seen concerted international efforts to aid those affected by natural disasters; the recognition and an apology for the suffering caused to Africa by European expansion and imperialism; and the acceptance of the need for the world to act collectively to address the threat of climate change and global warming.

Whilst many of these seemingly altruistic acts may have been born of fear and self-interest, they have nonetheless, contributed to a sense of introspection, contrition and active social responsibility. Consequently, they have paved the way for something new.

As without, so within...

Historians will probably tell you that this is just history in the making, but for me, it seems to be so much more. In many ways, it really does feel like the dawning of the Age of Aquarius.

As without, so within

There is an old adage that describes the relationship between our outer and inner worlds that says, 'as without, so within'. Put simply, it says that everything that goes on within us as individuals is reflected in our outer world. This can be said to be true of nations, groups of people, as well as individuals. If we truly accept this idea, then what that means is that the big events that are taking place around us on a global level, are saying something about us and to us as a species; as a human race. Similarly, on a national level, these events reflect back to us who we are being at any given moment; and the small but significant movement from negative to positive exhibited in modern western culture, is merely such a reflection.

So what does all this mean? If, as I believe, the world around us is showing us, 'as without, so within', then we know that the social, cultural and geological shifts that have taken place in the material world in the last decade, must, to a greater or lesser extent, have been reflected in our own lives.

This has been borne out in my work as an energy therapist and coach, where clients, colleagues, friends and family have all been experiencing huge personal events that are changing their lives. The themes of death, divorce, redundancy and bankruptcy have all been very prevalent, and in each case, the sense of soul searching and introspection was strong.

What else did these personal changes have in common? They all resonated with the vibration of loss and the creation of space in order to receive. In the same way that the September 11th attacks in 2001 gave rise to a new introspection for the people of the United States; and the global banking collapse of 2008 forced governments and transnational organisations to act in co-operation rather than competition; on a personal level, these events enabled these individuals to start afresh. In their loss, they could come to terms with the new beginnings of life without a loved one; take the opportunity to begin a new career; and make a fresh start with the space to invite abundance into their lives. Whilst these experiences felt far from positive for the people involved at the time, many of them went on to do exactly that.

In this, the precursor to the Age of Aquarius then, there seems to be a shift in the focus, outlook and awareness in the people of the industrialised nations of the western hemisphere. Where there was once a widely accepted belief that 'might was always right', 'I'm right and you're wrong', there is now a discernible movement towards greater self-knowledge, understanding and co-operation. Change is definitely in the air; and this kind of change, in environment, attitude and outlook requires a different approach, and perhaps a different tool to work with. It needs a tool that falls somewhere between the purely spiritual and esoteric, and the practical and exoteric. The Circle of One is such a tool.

The Law of Attraction and all that Jazz

Have you noticed that when you're open and receptive to an idea, it will just come to you? This is true, not only on a personal basis, but also on a national, international and global level. A case in point being, the 'noughties' media phenomenon called *The Secret*.

It was 2006, and suddenly it was everywhere. Seemingly out of nowhere, *The Secret* exploded into our consciousness and onto our screens.

A twenty-first century science meets spirituality 'made simple' movie, *The Secret* described through a series of 'talking heads', the basics of the Law of Attraction. It explained how our emotions affect our energetic vibration, and how we could use this knowledge to attract anything we wanted into our lives; cars, houses, loving relationships – anything.

For those who had studied spirituality, and were deeply into the concepts of Universal Law, it all seemed a little too basic; too much of a quick fix. But for those who had shunned the esoteric in favour of the more worldly, it was something of a 'Godsend'; a wake up call.

For what it said to them was that we were not merely destined to be pawns in a huge chess game in which we had no say, but that we were conscious actors who could not only control, but command the game in which we were playing.

This was both extremely liberating and exciting. Suddenly, it felt as if we could have anything and everything we wanted, if we just focussed on it. Whilst this seemed to work for some people some of the time, to varying degrees; for many, it proved to be a disappointment. They had created the vision boards, written the gratitude diaries, and done all of the things that they were supposed to do, but they were just not getting the results.

What *The Secret* didn't fully explain was what happens when your emotions, created by the thoughts that you had been thinking for a lifetime, were deep-rooted, and seemingly contrary to what you said you wanted. Whilst it did give some techniques that you could apply that would help in certain situations, it didn't really seem to explain how to change those feelings at a deeper and more long-lasting level.

Yet in spite of all that, *The Secret*, in its simplicity had provided an 'aha' moment on a grand scale. The mainstream US media seized upon it, and chat show hosts, Oprah Winfrey and Larry King were both discussing the Law of Attraction, at length, on prime time TV. *The Secret* had made a lasting and significant impact.

However, what it appeared to focus on was what we could *do* and *have* if we consciously used the Law of Attraction. What seemed to be missing was the emphasis on the first vital step in the manifestation process; namely, who we needed to be. The process of manifestation is first 'to be', then 'to do', and finally, 'to have'.

Where the Circle of One differs from *The Secret* in its use of the Law of Attraction is that it uses the Law to help us see who we are being at any given moment, and to change it, before focusing on what we are doing and having. This difference is crucial.

When our motivation and drive is fixed on what we can have, our attention is externally focussed, and we are subject to the mood, condition or circumstance of the people and events around us. When we are internally focussed and our attention is concentrated on who we are *being* in the world, that is the only thing that matters, because from this, all other things are attracted.

The concept of the Law of Attraction, and references to it, has been around for a very long time. From ancient writings like the Bible and Bhagavad-Gita, to *A Course in Miracles* and *Conversations with God*, the message is the same: 'That which is like unto itself is drawn'.

Put simply, what you are, you call to you. Who are you being at any given time is what determines what it is that you have. There are no exceptions, no exclusions. It's the same for you whether man, woman or child, everything that's around you is a reflection of you; maybe not all of you, all the time, but definitely a facet of you, and by virtue of the Law of Attraction, you have called it to you. This is the basis for the Circle of One.

What is the Circle of One anyway?

Our lives can often seem like one huge confused mass of random happenings. People, places and events appear to show up in the most arbitrary fashion, and we do our best to make sense of them. Yet everywhere around us there are clues; constant reminders that help us remember who we really are and why we are here.

The Circle of One is just one of those reminders. It's a reminder for everyone, no matter at what stage of remembering they may be, that we only have to look outside of ourselves to see and understand what's going on inside. The Circle of One is a lens through which we see the world.

In practical terms, the Circle of One is a perspective, a model. It is a personal development tool to help us observe and interpret our outer reality in order to gain an understanding of our inner selves.

The essential premise of the Circle of One is very simple. Namely, it is the idea that we can heal the pain of difficult relationships by recognising that everyone around us is in someway reflecting a facet or aspect of us by way of thought, feeling, belief or behaviour. When we question ourselves and come to a realisation about the facet that we share, an emotional shift occurs that changes the way we feel, and consequently, our energetic vibration. Once that happens and we take the necessary action to discharge that emotion, we cease to be a vibrational match to the person involved and they either move out of our Circle, or they remain within it, but we no longer experience the previous difficulty.

In fact, the Circle of One is something of a misnomer, as what I'm referring to is more a sphere than a circle, where we are at the centre of a multi-dimensional experience that is replicated over and over again in our surroundings and relationships, and reflected back to us.

Just like one of those very big, very shiny glitter balls, if you hold one up to your face and look at it, not only do you see yourself on one mirror face, but you appear on many. In fact, depending on where you're standing, and at what angle, you seem to be on all of them at once.

In the same way that the glitter ball twinkles, shines and sparkles when the light catches one of its facets and reflects back the light, so too, do we. When the ball 'twinkles' is when we are irritated by seeing our facet reflected back to us.

When someone is rude or angry, selfish or afraid and we are irritated by them, all that has happened is that the light has shone on that facet, highlighting and reflecting every flaw in its glaring light and showing us our own rudeness, anger, selfishness and fear. Sometimes the light can blind us, and we cannot or will not see the truth that is being shown to us. But sometimes it shines just enough light for us to see that we are all one; many facets of one whole. We all make up the glitter ball.

Relationships and the Circle of One

The currency of the Circle of One is relationships. To see, to understand, to be part of and to witness relationships with ourselves and between others is our only means of truly connecting with each other. It is also our only way of really seeing ourselves.

In order to speak of a relationship with your self, or your body – you must first conceive of those things as being separate to you. If they are separate, then who are you? What is it that constitutes you? What makes you up? Are you really separate?

Ultimately, it's all about perception. It is never about the way things are, and always about the way we perceive them to be, and that perception is different for everyone. The point of relationships is to show us ourselves. If I declare that "I am Kuumba" in a world where only Kuumba exists, that in and of itself does not really tell me anything. However, if I say that "I am Kuumba" in a world occupied by others, I get to see my 'Kuumbaness' mirrored back to me. Kuumba only exists in *relation* to others. That is the point of relationships. In order to fully see ourselves, we can only do that in relation to the people outside of ourselves, whether this is our family, friends, parents, children or intimate partners. And yet this is an illusion. After all, we are all one. However, we cannot see ourselves by ourselves, so we have to have it reflected back to us in as many ways as possible, by as many people as possible.

So what difference does it make when we see? Well, you know all of those niggles, irritations and infuriatingly annoying things that we find in others? We would see that actually, the irritation is about us, and not them.

Whilst our egos might challenge this, our heart would be glad to know that this means that we have the power to change things. All of those conflicts, frustrations and misunderstandings that we have come to expect in relationships, wouldn't go away, but we would have a greater understanding of what was going on and what we could do to make things different.

Perhaps a parent or child, or an individual in an intimate relationship screams at the other, "You're not listening to me!" or "Why do you always have to be right?" They are both saying the same thing. They both want to be heard and they both want to be right. Rather than fighting to be heard at the expense of the other, all that is required is that one of them takes a step back and listens. By recognising and honouring the mutual need of another, each of them has it in their power to change the situation and consequently, their relationship.

Similarly, the same could be said of the relationships between countries. They are governed by individuals, so when the leader of a country stands up and demands from another that they are shown the respect that they deserve because "My way is right, and your way is wrong", they too are engaged in not hearing the other because they are too much alike.

There are those who would say that it is not as simple as that. Yet when we consider it, it really is very simple. What it is not, is easy.

It is not easy to show vulnerability or compassion in order to connect with another; or to trust that you have the personal power and freedom of choice to commit to being honest with yourself; and it is certainly not easy to constantly monitor everything you think, feel and say for the sake of your personal growth. Yet all of these things are necessary if we are to really see ourselves and make that change.

I mentioned earlier that the Circle of One, also known as life, gives us clues all of the time. We are never left in the dark, as we often believe, as there is always a part of our reality providing a reflection of who we are being; giving us clues to guide us.

These clues can show up in the form of telephone or face to face conversations, chance encounters with strangers, incidents witnessed, or the experience of the energy of an individual or collection of individuals.

The Circle of One shows us how to interpret this information, and what we need to do with it. In Part Two, we will look at the fundamental principles that can support us in doing this.

Part Two:
The Seven Principles of the Circle of One

The Seven Principles

There are seven principles that underpin the Circle of One. These are that we are one; we are at cause, you are free to choose; the truth will set you free; everything happens in divine and perfect order; take notice; and take action. These principles provide a foundation to support us in applying the Circle of One in our daily lives, and serve as a constant reminder that navigation through difficult times on any journey, is always better with a map.

We are one

The first principle is that we are one, and everything and everyone around you is a facet of you.

This idea that we are one has been around for a long time. It has been proclaimed by many faiths and belief systems at many times.

If you grew up with a religious faith, you are probably overly familiar with this expression. So much so that it is easy to forget what this really means. The idea that each and every individual in the world is connected is a very difficult one to grasp, especially when you consider just how many of us there are on this tiny planet. It's not just difficult to grasp because of the magnitude, but also because the concept itself challenges who we believe ourselves to be; our very identity. My sense of uniqueness, of what makes me special, is my strong and sustained belief that you and I are different. When you think about it, I am only me in relation to you; and I am invested in the idea that I am separate. On one level, it seems that everything about us is relational, dependent on the juxtaposition of one to another. Yet this is not real. It is all an illusion. We appear to be separate and disconnected, but in actuality we are not.

In his book, the Divine Matrix, author, Gregg Braden, speaks of "a type of energy (that) exists that connects all living tissue that has previously gone unnoticed." It is this energy that is referred to as the Divine Matrix.

Quantum physics has shown that both we and the world around us are nothing but rapidly vibrating packets of energy, and the extent to which things appear solid or otherwise, is merely the result of the speed of that vibration. When something is dense, heavy or solid, it is because it is moving at a slower vibrational rate than light, sound or thought, and appears to be separate. However, this energy is everywhere, all of the time, and is only distinguished by the speed of vibration and the consequent illusion of disconnection.

In recognising this first principle, we can counter the illusion of separation and the focus on self interest that occurs when we subscribe to this idea. Recognition of our connection opens the way for us to show our compassion towards others, and they to us.

If that is the theory, then what would it mean on a practical, day to day level, to believe that we are one? What does it really mean to live with that belief? How would we act? How would we behave towards others and towards ourselves? How would we feel? What would we say?

If I believed that you and I were one, I could not condemn you; I could not abuse you. In fact, I couldn't do you harm in anyway. Why? I would only be harming myself. If I truly believed that I was one with you, I would know that everything you said or did or believed was only a reflection of me. I could not maim, murder, rape or rob you, because I would be doing those things to myself.

Similarly, I could not condemn you for your actions because I would know that in doing so, I would only be condemning that part of myself that I recognise in you. It is this last point that supports the application Circle of One, and is responsible for the emotional shift that is necessary for us to change our energetic vibration.

Oneness

You are at cause

The second principle is that you are at cause, and all change begins with you.

To be at cause is the most powerful perspective from which we can live our lives. It is probably the most liberating of all the principles. To be at cause is to take responsibility for ourselves and our actions; it is to determine our destiny in every situation, it is to recognise that everything begins and ends with me.

Many of us struggle with this, as it requires us to be so much more than we are used to being. The idea that everything that occurs in our life is a consequence of the vibration that we are emitting can be quite a challenge. How, we ask ourselves, can that be, when I am not getting anything that I want? Whilst it may not be what you want, it is certainly what you have asked for energetically and emotionally. Your job is to take control of your emotions so that you can ultimately live at cause all of the time.

Whether it be the notion that everything is 'up to me', that is, it is my responsibility; or it's all 'down to me', meaning that it's my fault, the idea that ultimate power rests with us can be overwhelming. And yet, this is probably the most liberating principle of all.

Living with this underpinning principle allows us to release the need to blame others and give up the feeling of victimhood. It allows us to embrace the opportunity to take the credit, as well as the blame for the things that happen in our lives.

When we give away our power in an attempt to avoid responsibility, we are at effect rather than at cause. Our perspective on the world is that things happen to us; not merely that things happen. We see ourselves as being subject to the whims of others, and believe that they are to blame for the things that go wrong in our lives. Simply because that is how we are accustomed to think, it can be hard to let that view go.

The Circle of One puts you firmly in the centre of everything. In so doing, it goes against what we are told as children. Remember this?

> *"The world doesn't revolve around you, you know."*

> *"You're not the centre of the Universe."*

How wrong they were. We are indeed the centre of the Universe; all of us. Children know this intrinsically, only they often don't have the maturity to fully interpret this, or the power to live it out. What usually happens is that the essential insight that we are born with is beaten or criticised out of us, until everything we do is about others; what they think about us, what they say about us, whether they'll continue to love us.

We lose our own voice. We learn to deny our own truth and to accept someone else's as our own. The Circle of One is about reclaiming that truth so that we may completely transform our relationships with ourselves and others.

To get the most from the Circle, you need to be ready, willing and able to look at yourself. By that I mean that you will be at a point in your life where you have decided that things must change; where you have committed to really looking at the relationships around you; with yourself and with others, and recognise that it is for you to create that change.

We often say that we are ready for change, but usually we are not. We want something to happen, to be different, but we are seldom prepared to do what it takes to make it so. When we begin to live our lives as if we are at cause, we understand that even the things that happen in our lives over which we feel we have no control, are in fact, things that we ourselves have created. When this happens, our sense of personal power increases, as does our confidence that we are conscious actors in our own lives.

You are always free to choose

The third principle of freedom of choice is the natural extension of the second principle. If you believe that you are at cause, then you know that ultimately, you have the freedom to choose. Whatever the event, situation or circumstance, you are free to choose the way in which you respond to it.

This principle liberates us from the tyranny of victimhood. Not only does it give you a sense of your own power, but more importantly than that, when you are not in a position to take direct action, you realise that by virtue of the thoughts you decide to think about that situation, you can choose how you want to feel about it.

In his book, *Illusions*, Richard Bach says that, "We are free to choose a different future and a different past." When I first came across this quote, I found it difficult to understand how we could choose a different past if it had already occurred. What I came to realise was that even the pain of a difficult childhood or the memories of a traumatic experience can be overcome by choosing to give it a different meaning in your life.

Nelson Mandela, a political prisoner, and former South African President; and Viktor Frankl, a Jewish concentration camp survivor, were both aware of this. Although deprived of their liberty and held in the harshest conditions, they chose to remain free men by virtue of their thoughts, beliefs and behaviours.

We hold power in a situation purely by recognising our freedom to choose at the most fundamental level. It is this recognition that is the point of real manifestation.

Everything is in divine and perfect order

To some extent, this fourth principle almost seems like a negation of the one above, in that it appears to resign us to some sort of fatalism. However, the opposite is true. It actually reinforces our freedom to choose.

The idea that everything that happens occurs in divine and perfect order is not at all fatalistic, but liberating. It releases us from the fear of getting it wrong; of making the wrong choice and suffering the consequences because of it. What the fourth principle gives us is the reassurance that we can never get it wrong. There is no right and there is no wrong. There is only perfection. Everything happens for a reason, and is just as it should be, whether we can see it or not.

In a way, it is like trying to complete a 1000 piece jigsaw with only a piece from the bottom left hand corner and no picture on the box cover to guide you. It seems daunting. There are too many things to work out, and not enough guidance. How on earth will you do it? You know that you have all of the pieces – everything that you need is there, you just have to trust that the order in which you piece together the jigsaw will lead you ultimately to its successful completion.

The same can be said of life. You start off with only you and your limited knowledge. Things happen. You have no idea that you created these things, but you did. You created them, and by the Law of Attraction called them to you; and as these events begin to unfold, so your life is created.

What happens when the thing that you have to do is get over your fear? What then? Ironically, the only sure fire way of countering our fear, is to do the thing itself. Yes I know, that's probably not what you wanted to hear, but that's all there is. Some snazzy, sexy, quick fix method that requires a little less of you would probably have been preferable, but as they say, "Them's the breaks".

The only counter to fear that I know is trust. Trust that you'll be okay; trust that you can't get it wrong; trust that whatever happens, everything is in divine and perfect order, just as it is.

Divine and perfect order does not mean you have no will to act. It means that when you act, you cannot fail. The real breakthrough is in taking any action. It is not about a guarantee that the action you take will be the 'right' one. As all action is in divine & perfect order, you cannot get it wrong. If we do not take a leap of faith and trust, then the fear continues to debilitate us and we remain trapped. The pattern continues until we take the action that will change our vibration.

This refusal to act is destined only to compound the fear. Ultimately, it is only in doing, saying, facing the thing we fear that we can truly loosen the hold it has on us.

The truth will set you free

It is said that joy, love and truth are all of the same vibration. That is, that in an energetic sense, they are the emotions that enable us to vibrate at our highest frequency and to more readily connect to the feeling of 'oneness'. Truth, in particular, is such a vibration.

This fifth principle is based on the belief that an open and honest heart will allow you to see yourself more clearly, and that you are free to speak your truth in the knowledge that every time you do so, you raise your personal vibration.

When we lie or exhibit some other symptom of dishonesty, we are resisting something, and this resistance blocks our awareness, our truth, and our growth.

In this age of relativism, there is always the question of whose truth we are discussing, but ultimately, what we are talking about is the truth that serves you; the truth that serves your highest good; the truth that serves your aim of remembering who you really are. What Neale Donald Walsch refers to as, "The grandest version of the greatest vision of who you really are". This is the truth that will set you free.

When we choose to ignore this, we end up painting a picture that reinterprets, misinterprets and misrepresents reality in our favour, creating an illusion that fundamentally gets in the way of us seeing ourselves clearly.

When we are busily living in our own world and living our own illusion, we seldom allow anything to interrupt that illusion. When we are living the illusion and telling the story, we distort our reality. What we see are distortions of what we think our reality is, or how we believe it ought to be. Our perception of ourselves is only that; a perception created by us; an accumulation of other distortions and delusions, and it is always fascinating to see us at work in creating them. The degree of exaggeration and embellishment that we employ in order to create, weave and 'get into our story' is often an act of pure genius.

We shroud ourselves in dishonesty, denial and self delusion in an effort to avoid the truth; our truth. Because our truth is often too painful, we trade it for another more palatable version. And therein lays the difficulty. For as long as we refuse to see ourselves as we really are, we can never truly grow.

It's a bit like navigating our way to a particular destination. If I want to travel from London to Birmingham, I must first find out where I am on the map. If I'm in London, there's no point in me pretending that I'm in Devon or Cornwall, because that will set me up for getting lost before I even start. Never mind that there's more pleasant scenery in Devon, and the genteel country image resonates more readily with how I see myself; I am not in Devon.

If I lie to myself and pretend that I am, then guess what happens on my journey? I get lost. And that is what happens to us everyday, all of our lives. When we don't tell the truth about where we are and who we are being, we get lost, and imprisoned by the drama that we have created. In order to free ourselves, we have to commit to telling the truth about where we are on the map.

When we choose to live our personal truth, and are ready to ask the difficult questions, we are ready to let go of our story. We are freed to pursue our spiritual expansion and to experience the love and joy that are a part of who we really are.

Take notice

The saying "As without, so within" is a truism that still manages to amaze me; largely, because its simplicity belies the huge promise and potential that it offers. What it says to me is, if you let it, life will show you yourself in so many ways. It will show you your strengths, your challenges and your contradictions, if only you would open your eyes to see them. The sixth principle is the embodiment of that saying.

In a way, it is enough to make you paranoid, but the key to this principle is paying attention and noticing everything that goes on around you because if you're seeing it, you're being it. From phone calls, to chance meetings; from equipment failure to aching knees, everything and everyone around you is telling you something. Your task is to work out what it is.

On a day to day basis, this could be very tiresome. After all, when something goes wrong in our lives, like the boiler breaking down, or light bulbs blowing, we do not really want to be asked, "But what is this telling you?" Especially as our first response is likely to be, "It's telling me that the bloody boiler's broken down! No more, no less, it's just broken."

It can be hard enough to deal with the drama itself without having to continually search for some deeper meaning. And yet, as annoying as it may seem, that is exactly what is going on. You are being shown something which actually does have a deeper meaning.

When you go through a period where things are constantly breaking down, or the level of clutter in your home has reached unbearable proportions, there is a message in it for you. The key to seeing it is to ask yourself "where am I being like that in my life?"

In the first instance, it could be that your energy is blocked, or you can't cope with the current pressure; it may even be a case of you needing to renew your energy source so that you can keep things moving.

The fact that you cannot get from one side of the room to the other without practically breaking your neck is indicative of the blocks that you are putting in your own way. It may also be a reflection of your head feeling full and muddled, or a general lack of clarity.

What is important in this principle is that we do not allow ourselves to become distracted by the detail, the story. Yes, the detail of subtleties and nuances can be informative sometimes, but largely, they obscure. They get in the way and stop us from seeing the truth.

It is when we take notice and focus on the 'bare bones' of a situation and how it relates to us, that we can really see what is going on.

Take action

By taking action you keep on moving, this is the essence of the seventh principle.

According to Taoist philosophy, the flutter of a butterfly's wing in one part of the world can have an impact on life across the other side of the globe. As we exist in a vast ocean of vibrating energy packets, any movement or agitation on our part in one area, will create a wave of activity elsewhere in the Universe. We are in turn, of course, impacted upon by the agitations of others, creating a series of what appear to be random occurrences around us and to us.

What this shows us is that movement and action are the stuff of life and are inherent to our existence as human beings. When we stop moving and refuse to take action we become stagnant and stale. This stagnation pervades all areas of our life, showing up in our relationships, career and health, and leaving us feeling stuck and unfulfilled.

It is important however, to make the distinction between taking action and busying ourselves in a constant round of 'doing'. We all know someone who is continually busy, but never seems to improve in the areas of their life that matter. So we know that meaningless doing is not the answer. Taking action is.

To take action is so much wider. It is about keeping the energy moving. Whether that involves changing our environment, changing our friends or simply changing our hearts and minds, it will create movement elsewhere that will inevitably touch our lives.

Up to this point, our focus has been on the philosophy and principles that support the Circle of One. However, the Circle of One is a practical tool and its strength lies in its real life application.

In the next section, we will look at how we apply the Circle on a day to day basis, and consider some of the issues that may arise when we do this.

Part Three: Applying The Circle of One

Before We Start

Before we look at how we use the Circle of One in detail, it will be helpful to look at some of the issues that can come up when applying it.

A question of belief

With any new approach we take, especially in matters of personal development, there is usually a certain amount of scepticism and some doubt as to whether it will work for us. If the approach contains elements of the intangible, or seems a little 'out there', we may be inclined to wonder if we need to believe in it for it to work.

Belief...

In this case, believing in or not believing in the Circle of One is almost irrelevant. I say almost because it would still take some element of belief in its possibility for you to bother to apply it. However, there is nothing to believe in, as such. You can apply the Circle, or ask yourself the question of, 'where am I being like that in my life?' and even answer the question without believing a word in this book about energy, vibration or the Law of Attraction. What is important is that when a situation arises, you first ask and then continue to answer the question. The answer is not affected by whether you believe in any of the underlying principles.

Using the Circle

You can use the Circle of One as often as you like. It can be every day, once a week, once a month or any time when you want to gain some insight. The aim however is to make the Circle of One intrinsic to your very being so you use it intuitively all the time.

One of the best times to apply the Circle is when you have had an argument and are feeling irritated or are particularly emotive about a person, event or situation. The reason for this is that your strength of feeling in the matter gives an indication of how much it resonates with you, and consequently, can give real clarity when applying the Circle. However, it is important to remember that in this context, when our emotions are heightened, we may be inclined to deny what is being shown to us, and fail to trust that 'the truth will set us free'.

If you write a regular journal, however intermittently, it can be useful to draw a Circle alongside it to get some clarity about what is really going on for you.

Who and what to include

Sometimes when applying the Circle of One, we may come across a person that we have lost touch with or we are not very close to, and wonder whether we should include them in our Circle. If you have not seen them for a while, and they have turned up now, then they have come into your life at that point, for a reason. Even if they are not close to you, they will still be exhibiting a characteristic or trait with which you personally resonate. They should also be included in your Circle.

Similarly, you may encounter people who you have never met before and consequently, have no idea of what their issues may be. Obviously, you cannot use what you do not know, but as this is all about *your* vibration, rather than theirs, your focus must be about how you are experiencing them; about how they feel to you. As we are often focussed on our thoughts, and what we know of something intellectually, it is important here, to make the distinction between how they *feel* to you, rather than what you *think* about them. Both aspects will have a bearing, but it is your perception that counts.

As well as people, you may also include a health condition as part of your Circle if it has started to become dominant in your consciousness. Energetically speaking, certain organs and physical conditions relate to specific aspects of your self. So, for example, if you have difficulty walking because you suffer from arthritis in the knee, that is also an indicator of your stiffness or inflexibility, and consequently, your inability to move forward in your life.

Free to choose...

Resistance

The experience of resistance when applying the Circle is not unusual, but is an integral part of the process. However, it is worth bearing in mind that just like the old saying goes, 'what you resist persists'.

There are a least three forms of resistance to the messages we get from the Circle of One. The first is when we see a pattern, but refuse to acknowledge it. The messages continue to show up in different ways and come through different people and situations, and they become louder and more persistent until we do take notice. That is what is happening when we find ourselves in relationships where the same patterns are repeated, or are in constant misunderstandings with others. Until we notice the pattern and do something to interrupt it, we are compelled to repeat it.

The second form of resistance shows up when we can see the similarities between us and the others in our Circle, but deny them in the belief that we are an exception.

For example, our first reaction when drawing the Circle is to deny its implications. After all, who wants to accept the idea that they are being unreasonable or hypocritical or dishonest?

We usually start off by saying "No" that can't be right because, "I'm nothing like that" or "It's different with me". The truth is that in any situation where there is even the slightest semblance to ourselves, we quickly deny and dismiss the likeness with justifications of why this situation is so different. Unfortunately, this is self-defeating, and the sooner we accept, the sooner we can shift our energy.

The third form of resistance is when we recognise a particular facet that may be embodied by an individual and we try to avoid it by avoiding them. Who and what we're attracted to, shows us who we are. Therefore avoidance of certain individuals just because we no longer wish to be associated with a particular facet of that person, is futile. As annoying as it is, avoiding that particular individual will not make any difference. Another person with similar traits or characteristics will show up instead. The reason for this is that it's not the individual that is the issue. It is the energetic vibration of the facet associated with that individual that is important, because that is what you share. When you are no longer a vibrational match for that person, that is, that you are not being the same as them, they will either move out of your Circle, or if they remain within it, that particular characteristic will no longer bother you.

Making an emotional shift

In between noticing the facets that we share with others and taking action, there is knowing what action we need to take. This is a crucial point of emotional shift, and it comes when we recognise the shared facet in ourselves; when we see and identify with what is similar in us and the other person. In that moment, we are released from our posturing, self-righteousness, blame and separateness to feel and show compassion. It is at this point that the emotional shift takes place. Often, this shift takes the form of four emotional responses; love, remorse, forgiveness and gratitude, and can completely transform the way we see ourselves and others.

When we say "I'm sorry" "I love you" "Please forgive me" "Thank you", or take an action that is in accordance with the vibration of these phrases, we reinforce our emotional shift.

About taking action

One last thing to consider is what happens once we have identified the facet, experienced a shift in our emotions and need to take action. For some, this part of the process may seem a little daunting, especially if taking action involves issues of conflict or forgiveness.

What does it mean to take action? Does it mean that we actively have to do something, say something, or write something? When we have used the Circle a number of times, we may not have to do this. However, at the beginning of using the Circle of One, taking tangible, measurable action is often a good way of moving forward, as it anchors the change of perspective in our bodies and minds. It is a concrete indication that we have made a shift.

Similarly, when we first start using the process, one of the questions that arises is whether our actions need to be witnessed, or is it enough that we know? Again, it is important to remember that the purpose of taking action is to change your vibration, so anything that you do that can reinforce the shift, is preferable.

How to use the Circle

Using the Circle is a very simple affair that can be completed in seven distinct stages, each of which is outlined below.

1. Draw a Circle.

Drawing a Circle lends itself to a different way of thinking compared to when we make lists or draw lines. It allows us to be expansive and creative, and widens our perspective. A linear thought process or perspective can be confining and restrictive, and can prevent us from seeing the big picture.

2. Map out who is currently around you.

Adding what appear to be 'spider legs' or branches, map out who is around you at the moment. This could be people you've met, spoken to, or have otherwise come into contact with. It could include those immediately around you; in your life generally or who you may have recently encountered.

You don't have to know them personally. You may just encounter them in a completely random situation. For example, a telephone enquiry, or house call from an engineer. What's important here is that they have come into your sphere, or circle of associates, however briefly. Your Circle can also cover any time period, so can include people and events that have occurred today, yesterday or even six months ago.

3. Bullet point their characteristics.

It's important here that you list up to six characteristics in terms of how you personally perceive them or their circumstances at the time.

It is important to look beyond the superficial and not go into the story. The story is not important. Strip it down to the bare bones. So for example, rather than getting into the story of your partner not doing their fair share of work around the house, and going into justification of your complaint, identify the trait – i.e. selfish, thoughtless, not pulling their weight.

4. Notice and highlight the common factors

Identify any patterns that come up, words used, and whether you see them as positive or negative You may find that you use very similar words, but for different people. Notice your reaction to them as a pattern emerges. You may also notice that you may feel some resistance if they are traits that do not match the way you see yourself.

5. Where in your life are you being this way?

Once you have identified the commonalities between each person, the next step is ask yourself where in your life do any of these apply to you. Where in your life are you being this way? This is probably the most difficult stage of applying the Circle, as it often requires us to look at some difficult and unpleasant truths. It requires us to go beyond looking at our immediate feeling of disaffection, to recognising and admitting to ourselves, the way we are, or have been towards others.

The Seven Spirals of the Circle of One

7. Take The Necessary Action

6. What is Required to Move On?

5. Where In Your Life Are You Being This Way?

4. Notice And Highlight The Common Factors

3. Bullet Point their Characteristics

2. Map Out Who is Around you

1. Draw a Circle

6. What is required of you to move on?

In recognising where you have been exhibiting the same traits that you have identified, you may experience a range of feelings, including love, contrition, forgiveness and gratitude. Once you recognise what it is, decide what it is that you need to do based on any or all of those feelings.

7. Take the necessary action.

Do whatever it is that you feel you need to do to put it right. Whatever the act, it needs to be 'witnessed', either by the relevant person, or if not possible, when you share the recognition with someone else. The fastest progress is often when we say it to the person involved. However what is most important is that we re-affirm our emotional shift.

The Circle – step by step

The Circle of One is better understood in the concrete rather than the abstract. In terms of our ability to understand its effectiveness, it is best if we look at it with the help of a real life example.

We will examine a case study in the form of Lizzie's story, and walk through how we can apply the Circle of One at each stage, using the events in Lizzie's life.

Lizzie's Story

Lizzie was a mature woman. Her kids had grown, her marriage had ended and she was free to choose to do anything she wanted to do.

Only Lizzie didn't see it like that. Alone and afraid, and with little formal education and limited work experience, she was scared of what the future would bring.

Lizzie had always had difficulty taking responsibility. When the going got tough, Lizzie was the one who got going to find someone who could take responsibility for her; someone who could do what she thought she couldn't; someone who would save her.

And if ever there was a time to be scared, it was now. Her house was under threat; her part-time job was about to end, and the only person on the horizon was her.

But here she was at 55, alone and afraid and there was no-one to save her. There was only her.

In spite of this, Lizzie had completed a project that she was particularly proud of, and after many fits and starts, she had developed the courage to get out and start to make it work for her.

With her newly found courage, positive things had started to happen, and it seemed as though the support she needed was coming into her life.

There was income from a lodger; help with her website from a friend; and she was due to have surgery on her knee so that she could finally get on with her life.

A day in the life of Lizzie

Lizzie was just about sick and tired of being messed about. Her lodger, Karen owed her a month's rent and she had been avoiding Lizzie. This situation of late payment, part payment and now finally no payment had been going on for weeks. Although there had been an extensive exchange of texts, Lizzie had not come any closer to receiving the money she was owed.

Lizzie was angry that Karen seemed to be taking advantage of her good nature and she did not like it one bit. They had sat down and discussed the details of the arrangement; everything had been agreed; and now she was dodging and weaving like a prize fighter.

When Lizzie received the text from Karen, it was the last straw. She was livid. Karen had decided to go back to living at home and would not be returning. She had taken her belongings out bit by bit, and very few of her things remained in Lizzie's house. As she thought about what this meant, Lizzie's knee began to hurt.

Later on that day, Lizzie received a text from her friend, Roger, who had helped her set up her website. He had asked to stay over for a couple of days while he was doing it, and had offered to pay Lizzie for the accommodation. They had both agreed a figure. After three weeks of silence, the text from Roger said that he could not pay her the money.

Again Lizzie was angry. It was not as if she had asked him. He had offered to make that commitment, and now he was back pedalling; just like Karen. Again, someone else was disrespecting her.

It had been a frustrating day, and the last call that she received that afternoon just added to it. It was a call from the phone company chasing Lizzie for a payment for insurance against identity fraud.

Lizzie had been very clear at the time of signing up that she neither wanted or needed this kind of insurance and had declined the offer. The company insisted that she had agreed to it and that she owed them the money. Following consultation with a consumer affairs adviser, Lizzie was told that she could pay under protest, but she still had to pay.

Draw a Circle

Lizzie is the primary focus of this case study, and so goes into the centre of the Circle.

Map out who is around you.

There were three main contacts during Lizzie's day, Karen, Roger and the phone company. Although the contacts were by phone and text, they were still significant.

There was also the situation of Lizzie's physical health. Her right knee was constantly bothering her. It was stiff and swollen, and became painful whether or not Lizzie was moving.

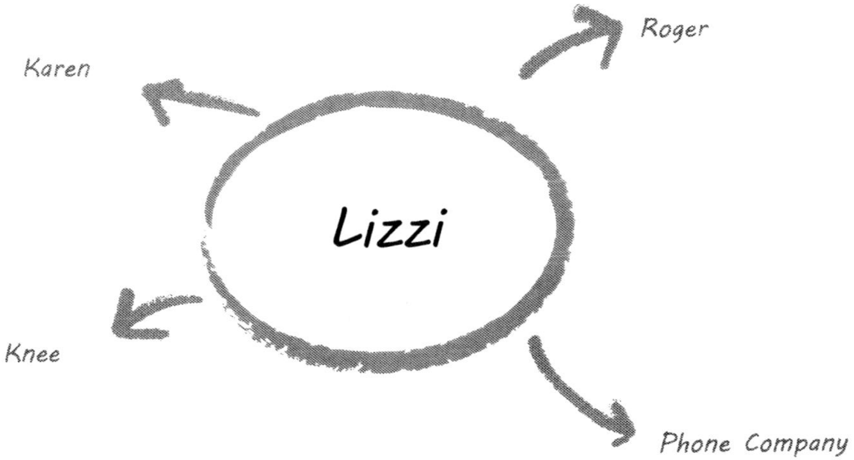

Bullet-point their characteristics.

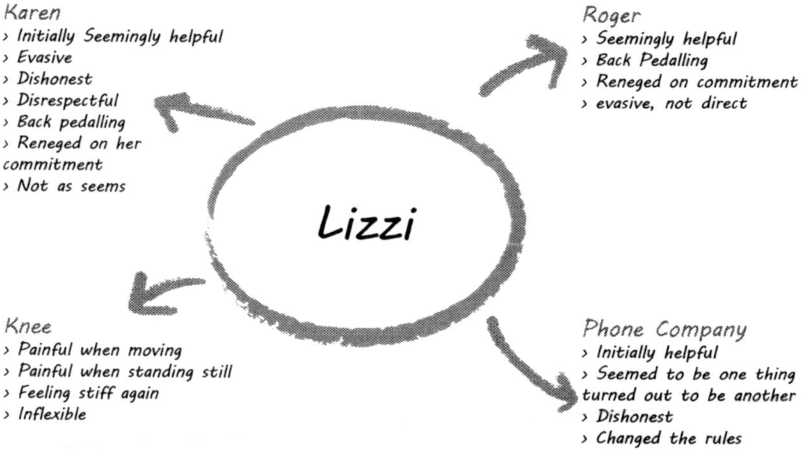

Karen

Lizzie thought Karen's initial arrival at the house was going to be very helpful to her, and that the extra income would help with her housing costs.

When Karen started to back pedal on the rent payments, Lizzie thought that she was being dishonest and reneging on her commitment. This was reinforced by the discovery that Karen had been secretly moving out her belongings, which meant that her actions were premeditated.

Roger

Similarly, Lizzie thought that Roger's offer to pay for accommodation while he was helping Lizzie to set up her website was also helpful to her situation. However, Lizzie thought that his avoidance over the previous three weeks was deliberately evasive in light of his text that he would no longer pay her.

Phone company

The phone company had initially seemed helpful when Lizzie spoke to them about their service, but their insistence that she had signed up to something that she had not, was for her, very dishonest.

Right knee

Lizzie had had surgery on her knee which was healing well. She was mobile and walking without a stick, but as events developed, the knee started to become painful and was feeling stuck again.

Notice and highlight the common factors.

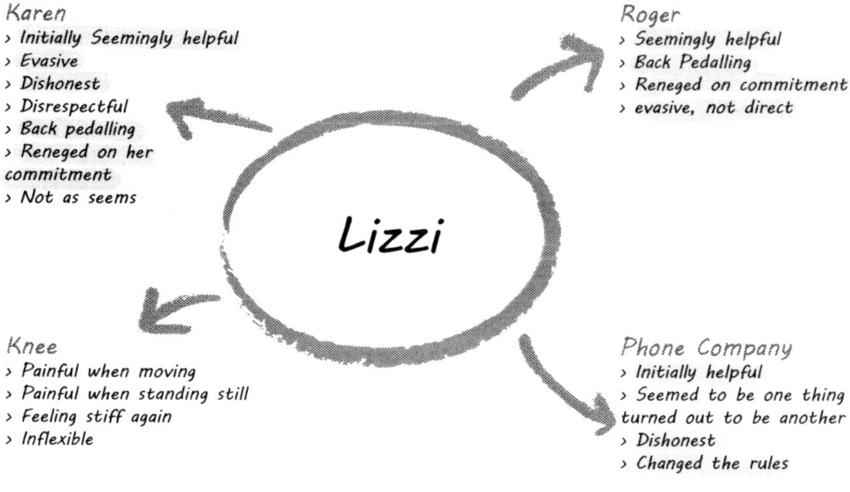

On completion of the Circle, the common factors were found to be:

- An initial feeling that the situation was of benefit to Lizzie.
- Dishonesty
- Evasion
- Reneging on commitments/ back pedalling

Where in your life are you being this way?

When Lizzie asked herself where in her life was she being that way, i.e. initially committed, back pedalling and dishonest, she realised that she had been doing this to herself.

She had initially made a commitment to continue working on her project and things had started to go well for her as she made progress.

However, when her operation date came around, Lizzie had subconsciously seen this as an opportunity to rest on her laurels and stop moving, in the belief that the income she was now getting from elsewhere would allow her to return to inactivity, where the responsibility for her livelihood became someone else's.

Lizzie was not honest in facing up to this and was blaming others for their behaviour.

What is required to move on?

All that was required of Lizzie was recognition of what was going on. She needed to be honest with herself about her part in the situation and make a commitment to moving on and taking responsibility for herself again.

Take the necessary action.

The necessary action that Lizzie took was in having a conversation with her friend and admitting to the realisation of the truth.

During this conversation, she admitted her part in the situation and reaffirmed her commitment to moving on and finding other ways to take responsibility for improving her financial circumstances. This would keep her at cause and at the centre of everything rather than allowing herself to become dependent on someone else.

Next steps

The knowledge and experience given by the Circle of One enables us to see ourselves reflected in those people and circumstances around us; to choose whether we want them in our lives; and to choose a vibration (thought, feeling, belief or behaviour) that is more in keeping and aligned with what we do want, and who we really are.

Applying the Circle to our everyday lives is by no means a difficult thing. The act of drawing a circle is not hard at all. However, what is difficult is reminding ourselves of the importance of living the Seven Principles in our daily lives, and the commitment we make to doing that.

In the next section, you will find case studies that illustrate this by looking at some of the issues that can arise in our relationships. Typically, these case studies generally only involve one other person, and sometimes, that is all it takes. However, as we can see from Lizzie's story, it may take the completion of a Circle showing us several relationships at a time, for us to see what's really going on. Completion of the exercises that follow will also help you to gain some clarity.

Case Studies, Insights and Exercises

Case Study: Finding Your True Value

Daniel was a self-employed consultant who loved what he did, and was extremely good at it, but never fully appreciated his talents in the way others did.

He loved helping people and struggled with the idea of charging what he felt deep down were very high, unaffordable fees for his work.

Eventually, the reality of the of cash flow situation finally hit home and he realised that he would have to increase his charges whether he wanted to or not.

He had been asked to carry out a service for a client with whom he had worked before. However, on the previous occasion, he had only charged what he called 'mates rates'. He was finally compelled by circumstances to bite the bullet, and ask the client for what turned out to be 3 times more than he had previously charged.

Before informing the client of his decision, he agonised about what she would think. Would she be angry? Would she stop working with him? Was he really worth that much?

Having finally summoned up the courage, he was resolute in his decision and informed the client of the new price. Whilst outwardly appearing to be clear and confident, he was not really sure that it was the right thing to do.

Over the next couple of days, there followed a tense and irritated exchange of emails. The client tried to re-negotiate a reduced price in what seemed to Daniel to be a very disrespectful 'take it or leave it' manner.

All the time the following story was going on his head: "That's so unfair. How could she take such an indifferent tone? She does not even care about my position. She is trying to devalue what I do. She is trying to devalue me.

What was going on?

The truth was that the client did not, and was not trying to devalue him; Daniel was doing that to himself. All the client was doing was reflecting that back to him.

The same way that Daniel didn't feel worthy or of value, was the same way that he had been treated. The reason he was really hurt by the experience was because it highlighted a facet of himself that he had never admitted to.

When Daniel realised this, all of the chatter in his head and his sense of victimhood left him. He told his partner how he had been feeling before, and what the realisation now meant to him.

When Daniel next spoke to his client, he explained the context of what had gone on between them. He spoke without feeling hard done by or somehow disrespected, and they agreed to disagree. Although Daniel did not get the commission, he was elated by this new understanding of himself and grateful for the release from fear, and the newly-found recognition of his value.

Exercise 1:

Think of a situation that has come up recently where you have been in conflict, disagreement, or felt aggrieved at someone's treatment of you. Were there any similarities between you and the other person? Was there a parallel situation going on elsewhere in your life between you and someone else, or even ways that you were behaving towards yourself? What were they? Describe them.

Case study: Being Used and Abused

Moira and Pat had been friends for a long time. Whilst Moira had considered herself to be a good friend, she had always felt as if Pat was something of a 'user'.

If Pat needed help, Moira was always there. Whether it was a shoulder to cry on, relationship problems, or any of life's disappointments; whatever Pat needed, Moira was always there.

This time it was money. Something had come up and Pat was broke. Her options were limited as to who she could ask, but she knew Moira was a safe bet.

When Moira received the call from Pat she was in bed. She had been feeling exhausted and unwell for days, and the one thing she desperately needed was the comfort of her cosy, warm bed.

"Could you lend me some money?" she asked, after a very poor attempt at feigning interest in Moira's ill-health.

"How much do you need?"

"Two hundred pounds, I'll give it back. It's just that if I'm late with the rent again, my Landlord's going to get nasty."

"OK then. Meet me after work tomorrow, and you can pick it up."

"Oh. I was hoping that I could get it tonight. It's due tomorrow."

"Tonight!" Moira screamed in her head. "Tonight! Why tonight of all nights? You must have known that your rent was due," she thought. But she said nothing.

"Alright then", Moira sighed. "I'll go to the cash point and you can pick it up in an hour".

"An hour? I don't think I can make it in an hour; I'm on the other side of London. Can't I meet you?"

Moira couldn't believe what she was hearing. "You're calling me at 9 o'clock, asking me for money, now; and you want me to get out of my sick bed, get on a train and meet you so that I can give you my money?" As the thoughts rushed around in her mind, Moira thought her head would explode. But she said nothing. After all, Pat was her friend, and it was for her rent.

So Moira agreed to meet Pat outside a station that was nearly an hour's train ride away from where she lived.

When she got there just after 10, it was raining heavily. It was cold and the biting wind made it colder still. Pat was nowhere to be seen. Moira waited. For nearly forty minutes in the pouring rain, with her head pounding, she waited for Pat to come for the money that she needed.

When Pat arrived, she didn't apologise for being late, or for the inconvenience. She just took the money that Moira held out for her; gave a cursory hug, and then left.

Throughout the train ride home, all Moira could think of was how used and disrespected she felt. Pat hadn't seemed to care about the effort that she had made, or the trouble to which she had put her friend. In fact, it felt to Moira that Pat behaved as if her needs were more important than Moira's.

What was going on?

Pat was selfish. She believed her needs were more important than Moira's, and acted accordingly. Moira felt angry and hurt when she did this. But Pat was only reflecting back what Moira was thinking and feeling. "Everyone else's needs are more important than mine. I am not a priority. It doesn't matter how I am feeling. Everyone else matters."

In putting her friend's needs before her own, Moira was emitting the vibration that she was not important.

When she asked herself why she was feeling so hurt, angry, and resentful, Moira realised that she was so busy taking care of other people's needs that she had forgotten her own. She had expected that her friend would reciprocate and felt let down and betrayed when she did not.

Having identified the truth, using the Circle, the next step was to begin her healing by speaking that truth, and to stop meeting other people's needs at the expense of her own.

Moira rehearsed what she would say in her head:

"I'm feeling very angry and resentful at how this has turned out. You are my friend and I didn't want to let you down, so I prioritised your needs above mine and expected you to do the same. When you didn't, I was angry. What I should have done was told you that the money was available and left you with the opportunity and the responsibility to come for it when you wished."

Moira learnt that in spite of any good intentions we may hold that "A betrayal of yourself in order not to betray another is a betrayal nonetheless". Such is the circular nature of these interactions.

Exercise 2

Look at the people around you in your life. They could be friends, colleagues, fellow students, members of a social group. Collectively, how would you describe them? What characteristics strike you about them? What do you like about them? What don't you like? What do you notice about them as a group? In what ways are you similar? How do they treat you? How do you feel when you're around them?

Case Study: Being Ignored?

Sarah started a new job. Her business had closed and after months of agonising about herself and her future, she finally conceded and got herself a temporary contract. As difficult as it was for her to make the decision, it was important for her because it was a way of giving in to circumstances without giving up. Money was tight and she had to do something about it.

The relationship with her partner, Mark was worse than ever as the financial pressures of the last two years pushed them further and further apart. Sarah was tired of feeling unsupported and uncared for, and had told Mark of her intention to leave.

Mark's inability to cope with their financial situation angered Sarah.

When she looked at Mark she saw fear, weakness and defeat, and she did not like it. She railed against it. She criticised it and condemned it. She condemned him.

In her new role, there was one person with whom Sarah came into regular contact. Her name was Hannah. She saw her around the building regularly, but despite Sarah's efforts to smile at her and greet her when they met, Hannah totally ignored Sarah; even to the point of not responding to her greeting and turning her back on her.

Following a relatively trivial event of having to vacate a meeting room so that Hannah could hold a meeting, Sarah was furious. "How dare she!" Sarah was angry not just at having to move, but it seemed as if that woman was worse than ever that day. Sarah was good and mad, and rang her friend to vent. Having worked with the Circle of One before, she knew that it had to involve her in some way, but she could not work out how.

"How would you describe her?" her friend asked.

"She's cold, distant, disconnected and rude!"

Immediately Sarah went through the various possibilities of who she could be treating like that. The obvious person was her partner, but they had spoken, and they both knew where they stood. She was sure it could not be him, but sent him an email and asked anyway. It read:

"Do you think that I'm cold, distant, disconnected and rude?"

Immediately, the reply came back "Yes! Yes! Yes!"

What was going on?

Sarah was mortified. All the time she had thought that he was the problem, when in fact it was her. She was the one who was being 'cold, distant disconnected and rude', and she had not even realised. She had distanced herself from Mark in an attempt to shake off the uncomfortable feelings that she had, so she would not take on the energy of his fear and 'weakness.'

What was really going on was that these were things that she saw in herself, but had refused to recognise or own them. Why? Because that would mean that she would have to look at herself.

Sarah was angry because she wanted Mark to sort them out. After all, they were his problem, not hers. He needed to sort them out, to 'fix up' and 'look sharp'. The truth was, she had neither the strength nor the courage to do it herself.

The feelings of guilt and remorse were overwhelming. That night she told Mark what she had learnt about herself, and apologised for the way she had been treating him. Sarah did not see Hannah in the building for over a month. The energy had shifted.

Exercise 3

Think of three people with whom you have come into contact in the last week.

Describe the strongest or most recently demonstrated traits of these people.

So this could be the characteristics you most commonly associate with them. For example, fearful, petty or the most recently demonstrated trait, such as angry; if you had or have just had or witnessed an argument involving them. Write it down.

Exercise 4

Now that you have seen the Circle in action, are you ready to apply it?

Think about what it was that drew you to this book. What did you think or hope you would get from it? What changes are you ready to make in your life? What relationships need to be healed? How have you contributed to the challenges/difficulties in your personal relationship? What difference would it make to you if they were healed?

Postamble: Squaring the Circle

If you have taken the time to read this far into this book, your desire for change is great. Now that you have discovered the Circle of One, and you are ready, willing and committed to using it, the challenge is to create a supportive environment that will ensure that you get the most from it.

As everything around you is responding to your vibration, so the key to staying on track is to keep your personal vibration high. Getting clear, being gentle with yourself and mindful of what you take in, and remembering that you are only human will all assist you in this.

Get Clear

Using the Circle frequently will help to give you clarity in your relationships with yourself and others. If accompanied by journaling, it will increase the speed at which you see patterns occurring.

Keeping your environment clear is also helpful. Take every opportunity you can to empty a drawer, tidy a cupboard or empty a loft. The sense of lightness and release that you experience will be worth the physical effort.

You will find that occurrences and insights come to you faster, as the creation of movement caused by taking action will have a knock on effect elsewhere in your life.

In addition to the above, if you have not experienced any energy therapies before, it would be a good idea to try one. My personal favourites are Reiki, Emotional Freedom Technique (EFT) and acupuncture. I find that Reiki gives me spiritual clarity and increased intuition; EFT works swiftly in clearing emotional blocks and past hurts; and acupuncture aids and accelerates physical healing. These therapies all work on the basis of increasing the flow of energy in and around your body, and I always walk away with an increased sense of clarity and confidence when I have had a treatment. If none of these sound like 'your thing', then the simplest, most affordable and most easily applied suggestion I can give you is to be still. Take fifteen to twenty minutes, or ten if you are feeling pushed, and just sit. Silence and stillness are the point at which we can connect. Clarity always follows.

And if being still is just too difficult for you, a good walk especially in nature is recommended. Ideally, you will do all three, as therapy, stillness and movement combined are circulatory by their essence.

Be gentle with yourself, but be honest

Nothing is more important than that you feel good. This is by no means a call to hedonism, but a reminder that the key to keeping your vibration high is in being aware of your emotions and what is going on with you. If you are feeling angry or hurt or fearful, then you need to acknowledge that. For how can you improve how you feel if you do not know your starting point?

There is definitely a place for targets, goal-setting and tough love, but sometimes we just need to recognise where we are, and decide to move on from there. It is not about extreme self-help or adopting the 'cruel to be kind' approach to personal development. It is about extreme self-care and being gentle with yourself. That increasingly loud and persistent voice that constantly bombards you with negativity, that we all have, needs to be told to shut up. Sadly, however, what we often do instead is to take in the negativity whilst trying to suppress the feelings that accompany it.

As we have been socialised to hide our fears and to protect ourselves at all costs, we anaesthetise. Whether it comes in the form of food, alcohol, drugs or sex, the idea is to numb our pain so that we do not have to feel the feeling. But feeling is the key. Once you have noticed the feeling and decided that you no longer want it, you can choose to change it. Your awareness of this and the honesty to follow through on it is the starting point for living your truth and raising your vibration.

Be mindful of what you take in

The best way to do that is by noticing what you consume, both literally and figuratively. So whether that refers to what you eat, drink or otherwise ingest; or what you see, hear and experience, take notice.

Where possible reduce certain foods like meat and processed foodstuffs, such as white flour and white sugar; and increase your intake of fresh, raw live foods like fruit and vegetables.

As far as drinks are concerned, drinking lots of water leads to clearer thinking and better memory function. Caffeine and alcohol dehydrate, so are best avoided or reduced at the very least.

Cigarettes, cannabis and other recreational drugs interfere with our experience of the world. They can impede our responses and impair our clarity so are also best avoided.

The suggestions above are by no means a moral judgement on whether you should or should not do any of these things, but merely an expression of what will serve you if your intention is to raise your personal vibration; in which case these things will help. If you do not feel that they will serve you at this time, then you are at liberty to do what works for you. They are by no means the only ways, but have been found to be some of the most effective.

In some ways it is a lot easier to notice the things that we consume physically. What is a lot harder to pinpoint is the myriad of overt and subliminal messages that we take in through the media, friends, family and colleagues. It is certainly worth paying attention to the feelings that come up for you when, for example, a news report on some crime or natural disaster saturates the airwaves, and is being constantly discussed around you. Such events can often take their toll on you and immediately slow your vibration without you having any conscious awareness of it happening. Once you're aware of the change in your feelings, take action. Change the subject, change the channel or just walk away. The choice is yours.

Remember to remember

I have often wondered what it would be like if we all lived the Circle of One. Yes there would be contrasts that may manifest themselves as arguments or disagreements, but inevitably, in the midst of any conflict, we would have to go back to asking ourselves that basic question, "Where in my life am I being like that?"

If we were living the Circle we would be continually calling, creating and attracting opportunities to grow, to short circuit the pain and accelerate our healing.

We are spiritual beings living a physical experience. In order for us to live out that experience, it is necessary for us to forget the wider knowledge and understanding that we came to Earth with, so we have forgotten; just as we were supposed to. Only sometimes, we experience fleeting moments where we remember, and we feel whole, connected and complete. I trust that those moments will increase, as The Circle of One becomes part of your remembering.

The Circle of One in a Nutshell

- We are One. That is who we really are.
- We do not remember that we are One and so believe that we are separate.
- Separateness is an illusion.
- The only way that we can see who we really are is by seeing ourselves reflected back in our many different guises over and over again, thus reflecting the whole.
- This takes the form of relationships and events in the world around us.
- By seeing them, we see us.
- Consequently we get a clearer vision of ourselves.
- This enables us to re-connect with each other, thereby reaffirming that we are One.

The Circle is complete.

About the Author

Kuumba Nia is a Personal Development Coach and Energy Therapy teacher who specialises in helping people face their fears, heal their relationships, and claim their unique place in the world.

Kuumba is the originator of the Circle of One Coaching model, and gives talks, runs workshops and coaching programmes based on it.

Kuumba lives in London with her husband and four children.

Further Reading

The Divine Matrix . . . . *Gregg Braden, 2007*

The Secret . . . . *Rhonda Byrne, 2006*

Seven Spiritual Laws of Success . . . . *Deepak Chopra, 1994*

Choose Them Wisely . . . . *Mike Dooley, 2009*

Infinite Possibilities . . . . *Mike Dooley, 2009*

The Hidden Messages in Water . . . . *Musaru Emoto, 2004*

Blocks . . . . *Tom Evans, 2009*

Man's Search for Meaning . . . . *Viktor E Frankl,*

Excuse Me Your Life is Waiting . . . . *Lynn Grabhorn, 2000*

You Can Heal Your Life . . . . *Louise Hay, 2009*

Ask and It Is Given . . . . *Esther & Gerry Hicks, 2004*

The Amazing Power of Deliberate Intent . . . . *Esther & Gerry Hicks, 2006*

The Law of Attraction . . . . *Esther & Gerry Hicks, 2006*

The Vortex . . . . *Esther & Gerry Hicks, 2009*

Feel the Fear and Do It Anyway . . . . *Susan Jeffers, 2007*

Loving What Is . . . . *Byron Katie, 2002*

Soul Coaching . . . . *Denise Linn, 2003*

Long Walk to Freedom. . . . . *Nelson Mandela, 1994*

Cosmic Ordering for Beginners . . . . *Barbel Mohr, 2006*

The Field . . . . *Lynne McTaggart , 2001*

Frontiers of Health . . . . *Christine Page, 2000*

The War of Art . . . . *Stephen Pressfield, 2001*

The Celestine Prophecy . . . . *James Redfield, 1993*

Tapping the Power Within . . . . *Iyanla Vanzant, 1992*

The Key . . . . *Joe Vitale, 2008*

Zero Limits . . . . *Joe Vitale, 2007*

Conversations with God Book 1 . . . . *Neale Donald Walsch, 1997*

Conversations with God Book 2 . . . . *Neale Donald Walsch, 1997*

Conversations with God Book 3 . . . . *Neale Donald Walsch, 1998*

Communion with God . . . . *Neale Donald Walsch, 2000*

Tomorrow's God . . . . *Neale Donald Walsch, 2004*

The Work We Were Born to Do . . . . *Nick Williams, 2001*

A Course in Miracles . . . . *Marianne Williamson, 2008*